1. A splendid example of a standard Gotha GII. Together with the GIII, the GII was the first of Burkhard's twin-engined designs and differed from the former only in interior detail. Small numbers of each type were built, and they saw limited use on the Western Front, one unit to be so equipped being *Bogohl III* at Ghent in Belgium. (Peter M. Grosz via Harry Woodman)

VINTAGE WARBIRDS No 2

The German Army Air Service
in World War One

RAYMOND LAURENCE RIMELL

ARMS AND ARMOUR PRESS
London – Melbourne – Harrisburg, Pa. – Cape Town

Introduction

Published in 1985 by Arms and Armour Press,
Lionel Leventhal Limited, 2-6 Hampstead High
Street, London NW3 1QQ; 11 Munro Street, Port
Melbourne 3207, Australia; Sanso Centre,
8 Adderley Street, P.O. Box 94, Cape Town 8000,
South Africa; Cameron and Kelker Streets, P.O.
Box 1831, Harrisburg, Pennsylvania 17105, USA

British Library Cataloguing in Publication Data:
Rimell, Raymond Laurence
The German Army Air Service in World War One.
—(Vintage warbirds; 2)
1. German Luftstreitkräfte—History 2. Fighter
planes—History 3. World War, 1914–1918—Aerial
operations, German
I. Title   II. Series
940.4′4943   D604
ISBN 0-85368-694-7

Edited and laid out by Roger Chesneau.
Typeset by Typesetters (Birmingham) Limited.
Printed in Italy
by Tipolitografia G. Canale & C. S.p.A. - Turin
in association with Keats European Ltd.

The German Army Air Service, like many other nations' air forces, evolved in spite of, rather than because of, the conservative traditionalists, the old generals and warlords, who were only able to conceive of modern war in terms of men, horses and cannon. Indeed, the First World War was two years old before it was possible to place German air units on anything like an organized footing and under those who understood aviation and could comprehend its potential effect on warfare.

Those German militarists who had prepared for a large-scale European war envisaged a brief campaign designed speedily to vanquish a comparatively ill-prepared foe, and as a result the deployment of aircraft was barely considered. When, however, the Allies halted the initial German advances, assisted ably by aerial reconnaissance, some members of the German War Staff began to realize the value of developing an effective air service.

When Germany mobilized in 1914, its military aircraft were organized under *Feldfliegerabteilungen* (Field Aviation Units). Each of these consisted, in most cases, of six aircraft, for use in reconnaissance, photography and artillery co-operation; at that time the need for fighting aircraft was not anticipated, although a few machines were armed. As the war progressed into a long slogging match, the German Army Air Service grew into a well organized and efficient arm, the *Luftstreitkraffe*, officially coming into being on 8 October 1916. During the following months, further re-organization established units in the field with specific duties, including combat patrol, ground attack, bombing and deep reconnaissance, whilst the number of fighter units (*Jagdstaffeln*) was steadily increased until, by April 1917, thirty-seven were operational.

Germany's air force saw action on all fronts and pioneered long-range bombing with its day and night attacks on England, first by airships and then, more successfully, with Gotha and 'Giant' aeroplanes.

With the signing of the Armistice in November 1918, the German Army Air Force was demobilized and some 15,000 aircraft fell into Allied hands. Today only a handful survive, cherished museum pieces serving as a mute tribute to Germany's first *Luftwaffe*.

For help with photographs for this volume I am indebted to several friends and colleagues the world over: Harry Woodman, Bruno J. Schmäling, Paul Leaman, Douglas H. Robinson, Phil Jarrett, Peter M. Grosz, Charles Schaedel, Colin A. Owers, B. Robertson and H. Nowarra; thanks are also due to Mrs J. Jones. Finally, I would like to dedicate this book to the memory of the late Peter Laurence Gray, respected historian of the Germany Army Air Service.

Raymond Laurence Rimell

◀2
2. One man and his aircraft. *Lt.* Malchow and this Fokker EIII monoplane were attached to *Kampfeinsitzerabteilung der Oberstenheeresleitung*, a single-seater unit established to defend the German 3/5 Army headquarters in the field. Note the 'riffled' effect of the metal panels, the laminated airscrew, the streamlined undercarriage struts and the machine gun. (Bruno J. Schmäling Collection)

▲3

3. An AEG GIV (serial unconfirmed) in wintry surroundings. Considerable numbers of these medium bombers were built during the war and the type continued in service up to the Armistice, some 50 still being on strength in August 1918. The AEG was used for night bombing raids over Allied 'back areas' to some effect, but its overall performance was disappointing. (Bruno J. Schmäling Collection)

4. *Feldfliegerabteilung* (Field Aviation Unit) *3b* during the winter of 1915–16. The rudimentary canvas hangars emphasize the somewhat primitive protection available to service machines in the field. Between the hangars and the aircraft (probably an Albatros) is a pile of wood which was used for signal fires to aid pilots trying to pick out the snow-covered aerodrome from the air. (Bruno J. Schmäling Collection)

4 ▼

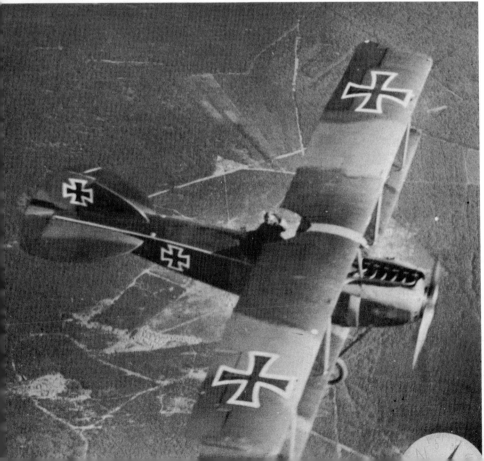

▲5 ▼6

5. The Albatros CIII two-seater was an operational general-purpose aircraft and one of the most successful of its kind; an example is photographed here by the observer/gunner of an accompanying machine. The CIII began to equip Western Front units during the winter of 1916 and was used mainly for reconnaissance, although if the situation demanded it could also carry a bomb load. The dark stripe seen on the fuselage is not a coloured band but a shadow cast by the upper wing. (Bruno J. Schmäling Collection)

6. A very fine air-to-air study of an Albatros CVII affords a rare view of the uppersurface camouflage colour divisions. Popular with crews, the CVII was used widely on reconnaissance and artillery observation patrols towards the end of 1916, and by February the following year 350 examples were in front-line service.

7. Albatros CX 9244 of *Feldfliegerabteilung 46*, flown by *Lts.* Geiger and Filbig – note the lightning bolt marking just forward of the fuselage cross. The CX succeeded the CVII into service during 1917 and was built by no fewer than four sub-contractors. A larger and more powerful machine than its predecessor, the CX could achieve a high ceiling and had provision for oxygen equipment for the crew. (Bruno J. Schmäling Collection)

8. What the well dressed German fighter pilot wore in the First World War: Ritter von Greim stands before a light-coloured Fokker DVII. The cumbersome clothing and heavy scarf were essential for long patrols in an aircraft with an open cockpit; there was, of course, no provision for any form of internal heating at that time. (Harry Woodman Collection)

9. A popular picture postcard widely distributed in Germany, showing the crew of an Albatros CIX two-seater preparing to take an extra passenger aboard. A few pilots on both sides of the lines often took their mascots with them on patrol, perhaps as some form of talisman. The animals' feelings can best be imagined, especially in dogfights . . .

7▲   8▼   9▼

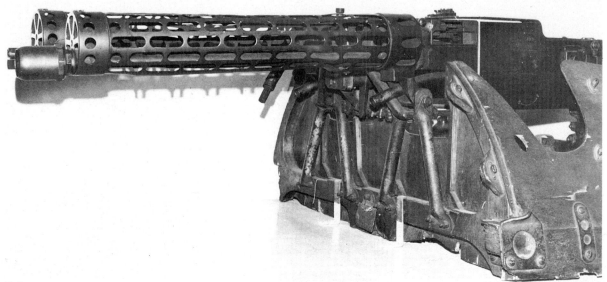

▲10

10. A pair of LMG 08/15 machine guns – the so-called 'Spandaus' – of an Albatros D-type fighter, as displayed at London's Imperial War Museum. This armament was standard on virtually all D-type and Dr-type German fighters from mid-1916 onwards, the guns normally being mounted singly on two-seater machines.

11. Albatros DII fighter biplanes of *Jagdstaffel 14*. These aircraft, a direct development of the DI, were, with their twin synchronized machine guns, an effective addition to the German air arm, and by 1916 over 200 examples were in service with front-line units. (Harry Woodman Collection)

12. Albatros DIII D2052/16 of *Jasta 29*, flown by *Lt.* von Budde, wears the stylized initial of its pilot's surname on fuselage sides and top. During April 1917, German units operating the DIII took a heavy toll of RFC machines, most of which were inferior to the shark-like fighter biplane. The windscreen of this aircraft is of a larger area than standard. (Bruno J. Schmäling Collection)

▼11

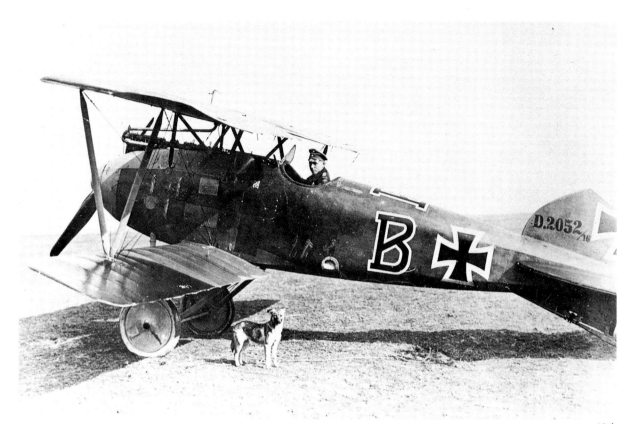

▲13

13. A rare photograph of an Albatros DIII coming in to land over the aircraft sheds at Boistrancourt. This particular machine is from *Jasta 5* and flown by *Lt.* Nebel – note the number '8' painted on the wing undersides and fuselage. This angle illustrates well the streamlined fairings forward of the lower wing roots and the wash-out of the wingtips. (Bruno J. Schmäling Collection)

14. German pilot *Oberleutnant* Kurt Wolff crashed this Albatros DIII on the railway lines near Courtrai on 11 July 1917 following air combat with Sopwith Triplanes of Naval 10. Other than a dark coloured rear fuselage (possibly green or red), the aircraft sports the standard finish. (D. Whetton)

▼14

15▲

15. Albatros DIII 2135/16, unit unknown, with striped wheels, a painted spinner and a 'sun burst' on the fuselage sides. A comprehensive study of Albatros colour schemes would fill a book far bigger than this one but, contrary to many statements, few aircraft were painted *entirely* in one colour; usually only the fuselage was so treated. (Harry Woodman Collection)

16. An ace from *Jasta 11*: Karl Almenröder, with his red-fuselage, white-nose Albatros DIII. Note the partially obliterated fuselage cross and the weathered, flaking paint beneath the cockpit. On this aircraft the red dope was extended to the undercarriage and all struts, tailplane/rudder and elevators being white. (Harry Woodman Collection)

16▼

17. *Leutnant* Oswald
Boelcke. A sound
instructor and an expert
organizer, with 40
victories to his credit by
October 1916, Boelcke
was one of the war's
greatest airmen. When,
as commander of
Jagdstaffel 2, he was
killed as a result of a
mid-air collision with a
fellow pilot on 28
October 1916, his unit
was renamed *Jasta
Boelcke* in his memory.
(Bruno J. Schmäling
Collection)

18. An Albatros DIII of
Jasta 29. Note the flush-
mounted radiator of the
upper wing, the leather
cockpit coaming, the
LMG 08/15 machine
guns and the grain of the
varnished plywood
fuselage. The flat sides
of the DIII are well
emphasized in this view.
One non-standard item
is the large circular rear
view mirror to the left of
the windscreen. (Bruno
J. Schmäling
Collection)

19. An Albatros DV of
Jasta 12; the markings
are black and white.
With its more stream-
lined fuselage, it was
hoped that the DV
would prove much
superior to the DIII but
in fact the increase in
performance was dis-
appointing. Vast
numbers were built and
the type continued in
production until 1918,
when the superior
Fokker DVII appeared.
To prevent wing flutter a
support brace was often
fitted to the interplane
struts and wing leading
edge, as seen here.
(Harry Woodman
Collection)

18▲   19▼

▲20

20. An extremely rare photo of an Albatros DV cockpit which reveals the latter's somewhat spartan contents. The tubular mount supporting instruments and the LMG 08/15 guns is prominent, as is the vital map and its holder (left). The guns were fired by trips mounted on the control column. (Harry Woodman Collection)

21. An Albatros DV with the British allocation number G56 painted on the fin, one of several examples captured and flown for evaluation by RFC pilots. One of these pilots was the ace Maj. James McCudden, who was unimpressed and surprised that the Germans managed to handle the aircraft as well as they did.

22. *Jasta 26*'s aerodrome on 4 June 1917. Front-line aerodromes

during the First World War were not too difficult to establish, and men and machines could be moved around as the situation demanded – hence the oft-quoted 'Flying Circus' soubriquet bestowed on German fighter units in the field. (Paul Leaman)

23. *Lt.* Arntzen poses with his Aviatik BI, No. 311, at a flying school in 1914. Both two- and three-bay versions were built, the machines being powered by the 100hp Mercedes DI engine. The device on the axle is a cable-operated claw brake, a landing aid of dubious efficiency. Note, too, the unusual form of national markings under the lower wing. (Bruno J. Schmäling Collection)

▼21

22▲   23▼

◀24

25▲

24. *Oberleutnant* Schonger and *Leutnant* Giegold of *Fl. Abt. 8B* and their Aviatik CI. The machine is armed with an LMG 14 Parabellum machine gun mounted outwards at an angle in order to clear the arc of the airscrew. The clarity of this picture affords rarely noted details: the airscrew manufacturer's logo transfer; the fuselage side radiators; the gun sight; and the gravity fuel tank. (Bruno J. Schmäling Collection)

25. An Aviatik, possibly a CI, captured by the French during the winter of 1916–17. The aircraft has been covered with tarpaulins and foliage to render it invisible from the air. The serial number on the fuselage is partly obscured, but a dark-coloured chevron can be seen forward of the cross.

26. A German kite balloon prepares to ascend. *Drachen* were used in great numbers for observation purposes and were high-priority targets for Allied airman; in consequence, balloons were heavily guarded with anti-aircraft batteries often supported by air cover. Although several airmen specialized in 'balloon busting', this was a hazardous occupation. (Paul Leaman)

26▼

▲27 ▼28

27. Instructional airframes of various types were used for teaching the many mechanics being trained for the flying service. The aircraft here are mainly unarmed B types, although what is thought to be a Halberstadt fighter can just be seen on the right, in the background. Note the steps and platforms for easy access to the fuselages. (Bruno J. Schmäling Collection)

28. A fine example of an Aviatik-built DFW CV. Introduced towards the end of 1916, the DFW continued to equip the *Fl. Abt.* units for at least 13 months, which was a lengthy period for a production run. Some examples continued in service well into 1918. The machine shown exhibits a pristine, factory-fresh finish – one can almost smell the dope! (Bruno J. Schmäling Collection)

29. Another study of the DFW CV. Of an unidentified unit, this aircraft shows clearly the printed camouflage fabric on the wings, universally known as 'lozenge pattern'. The DFW CV was one of the most successful of the many two-seaters used by the German Army Air Force, and Allied pilots justifiably held it in respect. (US National Archives via G. J. Balin)

30. This observer demonstrates the use of an early reconnaissance camera in an Euler C1. Note the flaking white dope of the national insignia, the pilot's rear view mirror, the fluted exhaust pipe orifice and the prominent wing rib tapes. The Euler first appeared in 1915 and was powered by a 120hp Mercedes engine. (Bruno J. Schmäling Collection)

▲31   ▼32

31. The 'lop-sided comma' rudder of the Fokker DII is well shown in this photo. The type replaced the Fokker monoplanes in front-line service wherever the latter were used in escort and protection duties, and as a result it never formed the exclusive equipment of any squadron. The machine is clear doped overall, with unpainted natural metal panels. (Harry Woodman Collection)

32. Fokker DII 547/16 in dark camouflage and showing narrowly outlined national insignia. Note the machine gun butt protruding into the cockpit and the leather padding deemed necessary to protect the pilot's face in the event of a crash. In practice, such measures would hardly be adequate. (Harry Woodman Collection)

33. Following the eclipse
of the Fokker E-type
monoplanes, the Fokker
DI was developed from a
series of prototypes
designed by Martin
Kreutzer. It was an
uninspiring and rather
mediocre machine and
only saw limited produc-
tion; certainly it was
markedly inferior to the
Allied fighters of the
period, and it was soon
relegated to the Eastern
Front and to non-
operational units. (Harry
Woodman Collection)
34. The Fokker M8 was
the production version
of the M6, which was
destroyed in a crash.
This two-seater Fokker
monoplane was first
built in September 1914,
some 30 aircraft being
supplied and used as
artillery spotters;
designated A1 in
military service, the
machine was powered by
an 80hp Oberursel
rotary. The A1
illustrated is a captured
example displayed in
London's Horse Guards
Parade in November
1915. (P. Jarrett)

37▲   38▼

35. The Fokker DV, in spite of its rakish, attractive lines, enjoyed little operational success, although it was easy to fly and generally liked by pilots. Two examples of this aircraft were held by the Richthofen *Geschwader* and used by its pilots to familiarize themselves with rotary-powered aircraft before examples of the new Fokker triplanes were received. (Harry Woodman Collection)

36. Probably the best-known aircraft of the First World War are the Sopwith Camel and the Fokker DrI triplane. Immortality for the '*Tripehound*' was assured by *Rittmeister* Manfred von Richthofen, the war's leading ace, who was killed in his all-red machine on 21 April 1918. This particular aircraft is from *Jasta 34b*. (Bruno J. Schmäling Collection).

37. An unarmed Fokker DrI of a *Fliegerschule* (Flying School), bearing large numerals on the fuselage sides. Although slower than other contemporary fighters, the *Dreidecker* was extremely manoeuverable and, in the hands of a competent pilot, could give a good account of itself against the best of the Allied fighters. (Harry Woodman Collection)

38. Two famous brothers: with a Fokker DrI as a backdrop, the Richthofens pose for the cameraman. On the left is Lothar, while Manfred adopts a characteristic pose. Both wear the *Ordre Pour le Mérite* around their necks, the so-called 'Blue Max' – Germany's highest decoration of the war. (Harry Woodman Collection)

▲39

39. *Lts.* Sternhauser and Wenzel stand before the latter's Fokker DrI on the *Jasta 11* aerodrome. The fuselage bands are believed to have been painted black and white, whilst the remainder of the machine adopts the standard streaky olive uppersurfaces and turquoise beneath. (Bruno J. Schmäling Collection)

40. Fokker DVI 1689/18 reveals a mixture of cross styles – not as uncommon as one might expect. Finish overall is the printed lozenge fabric, with metal panels and struts in dark grey or olive green. Only about 60 DVI biplanes were built, and most of these were assigned to schools or home defence units. (Harry Woodman Collection)

41. Unit markings on Fokker DVIs are rare, but they are evident in this photograph of a machine from *Kesta 1a*, a home defence unit. This view emphasizes the near identical engine/cowling installation of the type's DrI forebear, whilst the similarity of the wings and struts to the later DVII is also noteworthy. This Fokker bears the later style of cross insignia. (Bruno J. Schmäling Collection)

▲40 ▼41

42. Generally regarded as one of the finest German fighters of the war, the Fokker DVII was operated in great numbers throughout the summer of 1918. It was an easy, yet responsive, machine to fly and retained good controllability at its service ceiling. DVIIs equipped nearly 40 front-line units and were treated with respect by Allied airmen. (Harry Woodman Collection)

43. Fokker DVII 6825/18 in French hands. This machine is covered in the printed camouflage fabric, with metal nose panels doped in a dark colour (possibly green or grey). The DVII could attain a maximum speed of 122mph and was able to climb to 6,000ft in 21 minutes. Note the pale blue rib tapes on the lower wing upper-surface

44. Fokker DVIIs being transported on railway wagons, the interplane 'N' struts bound to the fuselage sides. Popular aircraft with pilots, DVIIs sported some highly individualistic personal markings as well as the usual colourful *Jasta* decor. The machines usually left the factory in lozenge fabric covering, with dull green or grey metal areas. (Bruno J. Schmäling Collection)

42 ▲

43 ▲   44 ▼

▲ 45

▲ 46 ▼ 47

45. Some famous German airmen, all *Pour le Mérite* holders, at Adlerhofen. Left to right: unknown; *Lt.* Veltjens (*Jasta* 15); *Lt.* Jacobs (*Jasta* 7); *Oblt.* von Boenigk (*JG II*); *Hptm.* von Schleich (*JG IV*); *Oblt.* Udet (*Jasta* 4); *Hptm.* Loerzer (*JG III*); *Lt.* Baumer (*Jasta* 2); *Hptm.* Göring (*JG I*); and *Lt.* Bongartz (*Jasta* 36). (Bruno J. Schmäling Collection)

46. *Lt.* Ernst Udet tests a Fokker EV parasol-winged fighter. This close-up shows the stencilled weights table over the printed fabric covering, the guide channels for the ammunition belts, the small windscreen and the leather cockpit padding. Udet survived the war and enjoyed a good reputation as a stunt pilot. He was a *Luftwaffe* general during the Second World War, and committed suicide in 1941. (Bruno J. Schmäling Collection)

47. A Fokker EV in the black/white decor of *Jasta* 6. There were some 80 EVs in service by August 1918, but structural failures and engine troubles led to the aircraft being withdrawn. Once the structural problems had been eradicated however, the type, redesignated DVIII, re-entered squadron service, but it saw very limited use as the war drew to an end. (Harry Woodman Collection)

48. An EV (113/18) comes to grief. The circumstances are not known but the cause was probably wing failure, which necessitated the type's withdrawal; two German pilots, one from *Jasta* 6 and the other from *Jasta* 19, were killed as a result of wing failures on Fokker EVs. The plywood-covered wing was rarely clad in patterned fabric but usually painted a dull overall green. (Harry Woodman Collection)

49. *Oblt.* Student and his Fokker EIII monoplane, 1 February 1916. The *Eindecker* was the first operational fighter to feature a synchronized machine gun firing through the airscrew arc. These aircraft achieved notable successes against slower, poorly armed Allied machines until the advent of types such as the DH2 and FE2b. Forty EIIIs were at the Front by the close of 1915. (Bruno J. Schmäling Collection)

48▲   49▼

▲50

50. A Friedrichshafen GII bomber. Built during 1916, the Friedrichshafen was a neat twin-engined design for its day and, untypically, had only two-bay outer wing panels. The plates fitted behind the wheels (just visible here) were to prevent mud and stones from being flung into the pusher propellers. The GII was reasonably successful and passed into limited production. (Harry Woodman Collection)

51. Virtually a standard GIII (the most successful of the Friedrichshafen bombers), the GIIIa differed in having less curved wingtips and a biplane tail unit. It was powered by 260hp Mercedes DIVa motors driving pusher propellers, and the majority of the aircraft were built by Daimler. (Historical Aircraft Archives)

▼51

52. Unlike his counterpart on board the Gotha bombers with their large fuselage cut-outs, the ventral gunner of the Friedrichshafen GIII had a simple aperture from which to aim his Parabellum machine gun at any aircraft coming up from below to make an attack. In the background, just to the left of the gunner's head, can be seen part of the pilot's seat. (Harry Woodman Collection)

53. PUW bombs slung under the fuselage of a Friedrichshafen GIIIa bomber. The rack is a simple affair with cable retainers around the bomb bodies – note the offset fins of the latter, designed to make the bomb spin as it fell through the air. Patterned fabric is well evident, as are two metal sprung flaps covering the 'step-ups' to the rear cockpit. (Harry Woodman Collection)

52▲ 53▼

▲54

54. Gotha-Ursinus GUH GI, first in a line of famous bombers and showing a curious disposition of wings, fuselage and engines that was only to re-emerge in postwar years with the RAF's Heyford. Designed by Oskar Ursinus, the GUH GI was built by Gothaer Waggonfabrik AG in both land and seaplane forms. (Bruno J. Schmäling Collection)

55. Gotha GIII 387/16 in unhappy circumstances. The removal of the engine panels affords a rare view of the 260hp Mercedes DIVa powerplant, showing the large fuel tank under the engine mountings. These early bombers were often painted white or very pale blue overall, making them extremely difficult to see from the ground when flown at high altitudes. (Harry Woodman Collection)

▼55

56. A Gotha GIV of *Bogohl III* with a dark coloured fuselage panel and shield painted on the extreme nose. The GIV and GV were the main Gotha production types and, together with the Friedrichs-hafen GIII, shared the task of long-range bombing attacks on Great Britain from 1917 onwards. As a day bomber, the Gotha was extremely effective until more powerful aircraft began equipping British home defence units. (P. M. Grosz via Harry Woodman)

57. The cockpit instrumentation of a Gotha GIV. Of note are the Cellon panels on the starboard fuselage side and that over the control wheel to afford illumination to the instruments. Also to be seen are the bomb release levers, immediately adjacent to the forward window on the right. (Harry Woodman Collection)

▲58

58. A well-known photograph but one worth inclusion for its atmosphere alone. The crew of a Halberstadt CLII prepares for a patrol; note the band of signal flares behind the cockpit and the rack of stick grenades. The observer is being handed fragmentation bombs for anti-infantry use. (Paul Leaman)

59. A Halberstadt CLII in for running repairs. Built in considerable

numbers, the CLII entered service in the summer of 1917; later reinforced by Hannover CL types, it was used mainly as a two-seat fighter to escort C-type reconnaissance and photographic patrol aircraft. However, Halberstadts were also used for close-support and ground-attack, and were highly effective in both roles. (Harry Woodman Collection)

▼59

60. Another Halberstadt, of an unknown unit, displays a stylized arrowhead motif. The characteristic fuselage camouflage consisted of up to six colours scumbled together to achieve a mottled effect. Note the bullet hole patches on the fuselage and the tailplane, carefully painted to represent British RFC cockades. (Harry Woodman Collection)

61. The Hannover CLIII, unusually for a single-engined machine, featured a biplane tail unit, which did, however, give the observer/gunner a wider arc of fire. The type became operational towards the end of 1917 and was a formidable opponent for Allied fighter pilots. Over 1,000 Hannover two-seaters were eventually built; postwar, a few saw Dutch service. (Harry Woodman Collection)

61▼

35

▲62

62. An in-flight study of a Hannover with its pale blue rib tapes prominent over the patterned fabric wing and tail covering. The overall compactness of the design gave the Hannover excellent manoeuvrability, and it enjoyed particularly good lateral control owing to its large balanced ailerons. (Harry Woodman Collection)

63. The Halberstadt DII was powered by the 120hp Mercedes DII motor and entered front-line service during 1916. An attractive little aeroplane, the Halberstadt supplemented the Fokker D-types which were beginning to replace the obsolescent Fokker monoplanes. There was no fin surface in the tail unit: instead, as can be readily seen, the rudder was supported by a pair of steel struts. (Bruno J. Schmäling Collection)

64. The first product of the Junkers factory was the J1, designated EI, whilst a development aircraft, the J2 (seen here), was given the same number. Built in 1916, the aircraft depicted (252/16) was fitted with a 160hp Mercedes DIII engine. The thin sheet iron which covered the aircraft was revolutionary, and later types were covered with dural sheet; Junkers designs were quickly labelled 'Tin Donkeys' as a result. (Harry Woodman Collection)

▲63 ▼64

65. The single-seat Junkers J9 (DI) was ordered into production during 1918, but only a few examples reached the Front for operational assessment before the war came to an end. The now typical Junkers corrugated metal skin covering was retained on company aircraft designs right up to the Second World War with the famous Ju 52 trimotor. (Paul Leaman)

66. The Junkers J10 (CLI), a two-seat version of the DI, was put into production during the second half of 1918 and was intended to replace the Halberstadt CLII types in service; some 47 had been built by the time of the Armistice. The all-metal corrugated dural covering gave a light, but rugged, configuration. The aircraft shown is 12921/18, thought to have been operated postwar over Lithuania. (Harry Woodman Collection)

67. A standard, factory-fresh example of a Junkers JI. The aircraft was constructed from duralumin, the crew area being protected by steel armour plate, and the type was considered one of the best of its category although, being heavy, it was difficult to operate from soft ground. A total of 227 Junkers JIs were eventually built, and one survives today in Canada. (Harry Woodman Collection)

65▲

66▲   67▼

68. An LFG Roland CII '*Walfisch*' being refuelled. This flying school machine lacks armament but still retains all the fittings for the two machine guns. Produced as early as 1915, the Roland exhibited many features ahead of its time: a semi-monocoque fuselage, simple 'I' struts, faired-in wing roots and large celluloid fuselage windows to improve visibility. The device on the upper wing between the men is a crash pylon. (Bruno J. Schmäling Collection)

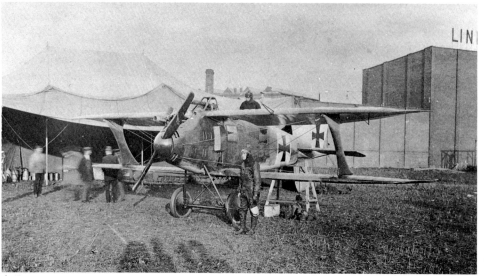

▲69

▲70　▼71

69. Another camouflaged Roland CII, this one armed. Note the bomb racks under the fuselage, the 'ear'-type fuselage side radiators, the crash pylon and the axle claw brake. The deep-bellied, streamlined form of the fuselage is shown to advantage in a view which also emphasizes the clean installation of the Mercedes DIII engine. (Harry Woodman Collection)

70. The LFG Roland DII was developed from the two-seater 'Walfisch' and, like its predecessor, was an attractive looking machine. Although quite speedy, Roland single-seater fighters were not popular with their pilots owing to the heaviness of the controls, a serious disadvantage in combat. Photographs of Rolands bearing personal markings are rare and, unfortunately, the unit to which this machine belongs remains unidentified. (Harry Woodman Collection)

71. This Roland fighter has a conventional centre-section mounting using struts instead of the more usual integral fuselage 'pylon'. Note the generous proportions of the fuselage and tailplane insignia, the wing-mounted gravity tanks, and the rear undercarriage legs passing through the lower wing roots. (Bruno J. Schmäling Collection)

72. Despite the evidence of this illustration, the LFG Roland DVI boasted a good all-round performance. The fuselage was of 'clinker' construction with parallel plywood strips, an intricate, non-standard form of building which was probably one of the reasons why the type was not produced in greater numbers. (Harry Woodman Collection)
73. A factory-fresh LFG Roland DVIb, numbered 5117/18. The planked fuselage was built to boat construction standards, using slightly tapered spruce strips of wedge-shaped section and overlapping one another by some two-thirds of their widths to give a smooth internal surface. The strips were pinned and glued to the light basic fuselage structure of spruce longerons and ply formers. (Harry Woodman Collection)
74. An LVG CII over the lines. The aircraft appeared towards the end of 1915 and was employed by all types of units, from the *Kampfgeschwadern*, where it was used for light bombing, to the *Fl. Abt.* squadrons, where it was employed on tactical reconnaissance, photo-reconnaissance and general duties. Some 250 CI and CII machines were in front-line service by the spring of 1916. (Bruce Robertson)

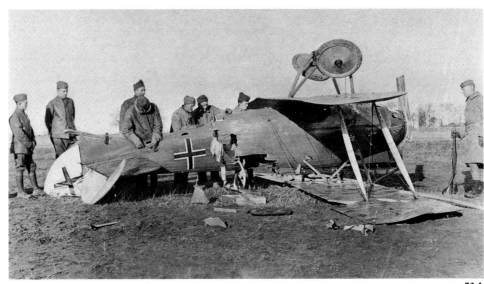

72▲

73▲   74▼

▲75 ▼76

75. An Euler-built LVG BII, 1013/15. Although the type was initially armed with only a Parabellum gun for the observer/gunner, later LVGs had their firepower increased by the addition of a fixed, forward-firing 'Spandau'. Production numbers for the CII have gone unrecorded, but the aircraft was built under licence by both Ago and Otto. (Harry Woodman Collection)

76. A fine study of LVG CII 4243/15. Note the upperwing-mounted radiator, the gravity fuel tank, and the rear-view mirror on the forward starboard centre-section strut; also noteworthy are the enormous windscreen, and the U-clamp on the rear starboard centre-section strut to secure the muzzle of the Parabellum machine gun when not in use. (Bruno J. Schmäling Collection)

77. Two members of *Fliegerersatzabteilung 3* study a map prior to boarding their LVG CII. Typical of many German training machines, the fuselage bears the school's telephone number, just visible above the serial. Styles of flying coats and helmets may be noted. (Bruno J. Schmäling Collection)

78. A camouflaged LVG CIV, number 267/16. The CIV was a slightly enlarged version of the CII, designed around the 220hp Mercedes DIV motor, the reduction gearing of this 'straight-eight' engine enabling it to be virtually fully enclosed within the fuselage. A slow-revolving airscrew of massive dimensions was installed, whilst the balanced rudder was a 'first' for LVG. It was an aircraft of this type that made the first daylight aeroplane raid on London, on 28 November 1916. (Bruno J. Schmäling Collection)

▲79   ▼80

81 ▲

79. The LVG CV was one of the most successful two-seaters used during the second half of the war on reconnaissance and artillery observation duties. Introduced during 1917, the CV, whilst not as powerful as its high-flying Rumpler contemporaries, more than filled the requirement for a reliable and stable general-purpose machine. Note the fully cowled engine. (Harry Woodman Collection)

80. An interesting glimpse into an LVG CV pilot's and observer/gunner's cockpits. An unusual feature is the gun mounting bracket, which is similar to the British Scarff ring unit; the curved 'V's either side of the wooden ring are supports for the gunner. Note the rudimentary instrumentation for the pilot. (Harry Woodman Collection)

81. Following the CV, the LVG CVI entered service during 1918, and some 1,000 were built by the time of the Armistice. It was of the same basic design as its predecessor, but it was somewhat lighter and the engine was only semi-enclosed. The unit to which this particular CVI belonged has not been recorded. (US National Archives via George J. Balin)

82. Aircraft undergoing overhaul inside a Zeppelin hangar. In the background is a Staaken 'Giant' bomber, and to the right an Albatros B-type. The other machine is LVG CV 1766/18 in standard green/lilac camouflage finish. The white area of the fuselage cross is of non-standard proportions (as is the large serial number), and the engine cowls have been removed. (P. M. Grosz via Harry Woodman)

82 ▼

▲83 ▼84

83. These LVGs exhibit a wide variety of exhaust styles. The CVI's lighter weight (almost 1cwt less than the CV) contributed greatly to the type's improved performance. Today, a superbly restored LVG is part of the Shuttleworth Collection at Old Warden and is the only genuine airworthy German First World War two-seater in the world. (Harry Woodman Collection)

84. Perhaps the most elegant of all the German D-types was the Pfalz DIII. The overturned example shown is 4058/17 of *Jasta 15*, flown by *Lt.* Schwabe. The DIII entered front-line service in the autumn of 1917, mainly with Bavarian units, and often formed partial deployments with Albatros and Roland fighters. Pfalz fighters left the factory in overall aluminium doped finish. (Bruno J. Schmäling Collection)

85. *Lt.* Heldman of *Jasta 10* is helped out of his flying clothes. The Pfalz DIII behind him has had its uppersurfaces camouflaged in lilac and green dope, but the aluminium finish has been retained on the undersurfaces. Allied reports on a captured Pfalz were extremely favourable, tending to refute the general view that the type was unpopular with German pilots owing to its alleged inferiority. (Bruno J. Schmäling Collection)

86. A Pfalz DIII, from an unidentified unit but reputedly being flown by *Lt.* Werner Voss, comes into land; the well-proportioned, streamlined appearance of the type is seen to advantage in this rare flying shot. The downward pointing exhaust pipe on the port side is clearly visible. (Harry Woodman Collection)

▲87

87. A captured Pfalz DIIIa in American hands. The DIIIa appeared in 1918 and was powered by a Mercedes DIII engine of 180hp; it also featured a tailplane of increased area, lower wing tip shapes modified to a more rounded configuration, and twin guns mounted outside the fuselage (thus affording easy access in case of malfunction). (Philip Jarrett)

88. The cockpit of a Pfalz DIIIa, number 1285/18. The twin machine guns were buried in the fuselage of the DIII and were heavily criticized by pilots as being inaccessible in an emergency. The instrumentation in the Pfalz was fairly limited, as this view shows. Note the one-piece 'U' centre-section struts and semi-cowled engine.

89. A Pfalz DXII of *Jasta 35b*. This aircraft was overshadowed in service by the popular Fokker DVII, yet the Pfalz was an equally good machine and in a diving capacity, at least, it was superior. However, the double-bay wing cellule and its associated rigging was unpopular with ground crews because of the extra maintenance

work it made. By October 1918 there were 180 Pfalz DXIIs in service. (Bruno J. Schmäling Collection)

90. The Pfalz DXII was supplied to *Jastas 23, 32, 34, 35, 64, 65, 66, 77, 78* and *81* as well as a number of home defence units (*Kestas*). There is little doubt that the DXII was a sound aircraft, and had the war lasted longer it would perhaps have emerged from the shadow of the DVII to become the standard front-line fighter. The example shown is a beautifully restored original preserved in Australia.

91. The influence of the French Morane Saulnier monoplanes is easily appreciated in this view of a Pfalz EI – indeed, the type was actually a slightly modified, licence-built version of the MS Type H. Some 60 EIs were eventually built, although their operational use on the Western Front was comparatively short-lived. Not obvious here is the painting of national markings on *both* sides of the elevators, a feature peculiar to Pfalz monoplanes. (Harry Woodman Collection)

▼88

89▲

90▲   91▼

49

▲92 ▼93

92. A Rumpler B1 flown by *Vzfw.* Raetsch. The B1(4A) was built in 1914 and used for reconnaissance and training duties. Note the side radiators and uncovered wheel discs. The Rumpler was powered by a 100hp Mercedes DI engine and could attain a speed of about 90mph. (Harry Woodman Collection)

93. Pupils undergoing machine-gun training on a Rumpler CI. The aircraft was one of the best and most popular of its type and first appeared during 1915. As well as Western Front service, Rumplers were also used in the Macedonian, Palestine and Salonika theatres during 1917. (Bruno J. Schmäling Collection)

94. Another Rumpler CI-based trainer machine is this non-flying example mounted on a special cradle that could be rotated and tilted. Such set-ups were designed to train air-gunners – note the recognition profile/target on the shed wall. (Harry Woodman Collection)

95. A fine study of Rumpler CI 393/15. The upperwing crosses are visible through the linen covering, which suggests that these surfaces are clear doped rather than painted. Note the prominent fuselage fabric lacing and the degree of 'wash-out' on the lower wingtips. (Harry Woodman Collection)

96. Perhaps the finest of all German two-seaters was the Rumpler CIV, which went into production during 1917. It had an extremely good performance and could attain an altitude of over 15,000ft – well beyond the ceiling of most Allied fighters. This machine is in one of the factory-fresh colour schemes – multi-colour upper surfaces and pale blue below. (Bruno J. Schmäling Collection)

97. A Germania-built Rumpler CIV, possibly the 300th model off the production line, a view supported by the special nose decor. Rumpler CIVs operated mostly in strategic roles on reconnaissance and photographic duties, often penetrating deep behind enemy lines and relying upon their unrivalled high-altitude qualities to elude Allied pilots. (Harry Woodman Collection)

98. Rumpler CIVs in front-line service. This version with the faired-in spinner is the cleanest-looking installation of the Mercedes DIVa engine; other Rumplers featured a blunt nose and a plain airscrew. Most Rumplers had all their struts painted in the pale blue of the undersurfaces. (Harry Woodman Collection)

98▼

99. The final development of the rather unsuccessful series of Rumpler twin-engined bombers, the Rumpler GIII (6G2) followed previous designs but the engine nacelles were cleaned up and raised above the lower wings by struts. Note the large pointed spinner and clean engine installation. (Harry Woodman Collection)

100. The German Army Airship Division played a promising part in the early raids on England but following the destruction of the Schütte Lanz *SL11* over Cuffley, Hertfordshire, on 3 September 1916 by Lt. W. L. Robinson, it was soon disbanded. This is *SL13*, *SL11*'s sister-ship, seen here during a transfer flight from Leipzig to Hannover on 19 October 1916. (G. Blasweiler via D. H. Robinson)

101. One of the best photos ever taken from a military airship. This view of the Army Schütte Lanz *SL13* is from the rear of the control gondola, looking towards the tail. Note the rows of bomb shutters running down the centre of the hull, the engine gondola's retractable radiators, and the ladder to the keel. (G. Blasweiler via D. H. Robinson)

▲99 ▼100

101▶

▲102

102. The Siemens Schuckert DI was a virtual copy of the French Nieuport 11 design, differing only in the installation of the engine and, later on, its tailskid configuration. Small numbers saw limited service with a few front-line units, but the aircraft was soon superseded by aircraft of improved performance. (Harry Woodman Collection)

103. Siemens Schuckert DI 3506/17 of *Jasta* 7, circa February 1917. This fully camouflaged machine carries a spinner and a comparatively large airscrew. Powered by a 110hp Siemens-Halske Sh 1 rotary engine, the SS DI could attain a top speed of around 96mph. Note the high-gloss finish of the wing surfaces. (Harry Woodman Collection)

▼103

104. This squat little aeroplane is one of the early prototypes of the Siemens Schuckert DIII and DIV aircraft, which many air historians consider to have been the best German fighters to reach operational status. For some reason, the aircraft continued to be manufactured until the summer of 1919, and at least one DIV survived until 1926 in Germany. (Paul Leaman)

105. Siemens Schuckert DIII 1611/18, flown by *Lt.* Kessler of *Kesta 4b*. The attire of the intrepid, bespectacled airman is of note, as are the fuselage insignia and heavy padding for the machine guns. The colours of the aircraft are not known, but the wings and fin are covered in patterned fabric and the rudder is white. (Harry Woodman Collection)

▲106

106. The curious Siemens Schuckert *Steffen* RI was one of the more unusual shapes to be seen in the air. Seven of these 'fork-tailed' RI giants were built; this aircraft is RI/15, which first flew in May 1915 but did not see operational service. All three of the aircraft's engines were installed in the nose, the power being transmitted to the two airscrews through a series of shafts and gears. (Harry Woodman Collection)

107. A close-up view of the SSW RI reveals the prominent radiators fitted to the nose and the extensive Cellon cabin windscreen and windows. Note the opposing pitch of the airscrews and the substantial rigging cables. (Harry Woodman Collection)

108. The enormous Siemens Schuckert RVIII R23/16 had six

▼107

engines, and although construction began in February 1918 the behemoth's first trials were not held until early 1919. In the event the transmission gear failed, one of the propellers disintegrating and heavily damaging the airframe, which, owing to Armistice stipulations, was not rebuilt. (Harry Woodman Collection)

109. The most successful of all the giant 'R-planes' produced by Germany were those of the Zeppelin-Staaken type; this is RIV 12/15, coming in to land. In its original form, as here, the machine was clear doped overall and carried national markings in large white boxes; later, when wing gun positions were fitted, multi-coloured polygons were applied over the fabric and the crosses changed to straight-sided configuration. (Harry Woodman Collection)

▲110　▼111

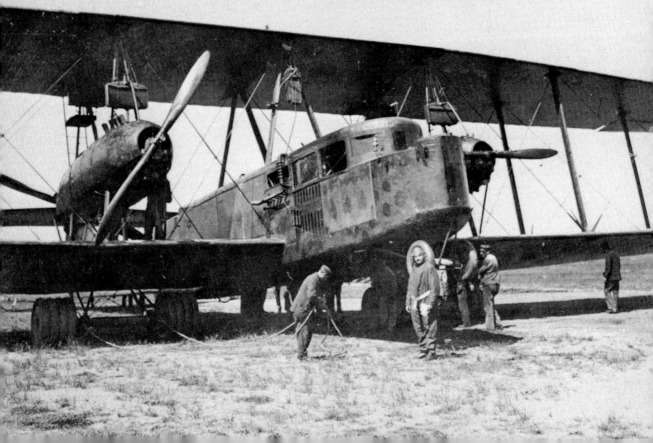

110. The Zeppelin Staaken RV 13/15 was similar to the previous machine but had streamlined engine nacelles and an upperwing gun position. This view shows a mechanic and gunner at their stations in the port engine nacelle, probably one of the warmest, and noisiest, positions on board the aircraft. Note the large radiators mounted on the 'V' struts. (Harry Woodman Collection)

111. The best known of the 'R-planes' were the RVIs, of which eighteen were completed; all except R30 (seen here) saw operational service. 'Giants' were used to support Gotha night attacks on London, and not one fell to the defending aircraft. R30 was a specially modified aircraft that carried a supercharger and adjustable-pitch airscrews. (Harry Woodman Collection)

112. A good, detailed close-up of the port engine nacelle of Staaken

RVI 27/16. Built by Schütte Lanz, this aircraft was commanded by *Hptm.* Schoeller on raids over England, but on 7/8 March 1918 it crashed in Belgium as a result of frozen fuel lines. The crew were uninjured and the engine and instruments were salvaged, but the rest of the aircraft was destroyed by Allied shellfire. (Harry Woodman Collection)

113. *LZ37* was the first Zeppelin to be brought down by aircraft. On 7 June 1915 *Lt.* R. A. J. Warneford RNAS bombed the Zeppelin over Ghent and it crashed on a convent, killing all but one of its crew. *LZ37* was an 'm'-type Zeppelin, measured 518ft 2in long and held a gas volume of 794,500 cubic feet. (Elias/Miller via D. H. Robinson)

▲114 ▼115

114. A Parabellum machine gun installed in a Zeppelin gondola. Guns were mounted in the main gondolas and above the hull on a special platform over the nose, although on later vessels another gun platform was installed in the tailcone just aft of the rudder. The gondola is of duralumin, with the upper portion covered in fabric.

115. The Army Zeppelin *LZ98* at Namur. This 'q'-type Zeppelin was built at Löwenthal and first took to the air on 28 April 1916. It participated in two raids on England, but in August 1917 it was dismantled at Schneidemuhl. (D. H. Robinson)

116. *LZ38* arrives over its base at Brussels-Evère in Belgium. To this airship falls the distinction of being the first aircraft to bomb London, on 31 May 1915. Commanded by *Hptm.* Erich Linnarz, *LZ38* embarked on several subsequent raids but the vessel met its end by being bombed in its own shed by RNAS airmen. (D. H. Robinson)

117. The crew of Zeppelin *LZ86*. In the centre stands the redoubtable *Hptm.* Erich Linnarz, striking a typical pose. This 'p'-type Zeppelin was built at Potsdam and its maiden flight took place on 10 October 1915; a year later the vessel was wrecked while landing at Temesvar and nine of the crewmen were killed. (D. H. Robinson)

118. *LZ97* is secured by its ground crew at Karlsruhe, 1916. The bow number has been removed for security reasons, and note the upper gun position above the nose. *LZ97* was dismantled at Jüterbog in August 1917. With the destruction of *SL11* in September 1916, no more Army airships embarked on raids over Britain, these operations being passed on to the Naval Airship Division, which suffered grievous losses as a result. (D. H. Robinson)

119. Tailpiece. A Pfalz DIII performs a nose stand following a misjudged landing. The unusual angle shows details rarely seen, including the style and size of the wing insignia, the wing radiators and the sharply tapering fuselage. (Harry Woodman Collection)

▼118

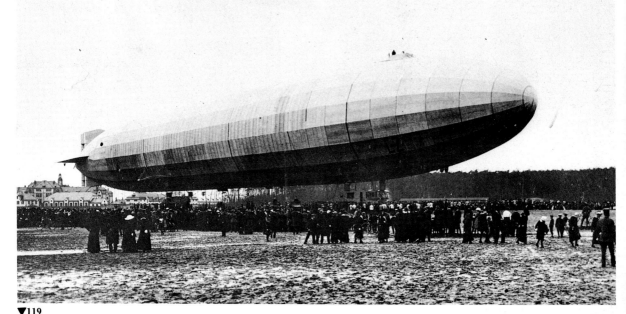

▼119